SMOKE

SMOKE

Poems by
Kevin Nance

Accents Publishing • Lexington, Kentucky • 2025

Printed in the United States of America

Accents Publishing
Editor: Katerina Stoykova
Cover Image by James R. Southard

Library of Congress Control Number: 2025942309
ISBN: 978-1-961127-17-3
First Edition

Accents Publishing is an independent press for brilliant voices. For a catalog of current and upcoming titles, please visit us on the Web at

www.accents-publishing.com

CONTENTS

Homecoming

First Light / 3
Gathering Tobacco / 4
Jacob's Ladder / 5
Under the Hood / 6
Mouths to Feed / 7
The Napkins / 8
The Right to Remain Silent / 10
Virgins / 11
Abecedarian for Adolescence / 12
It / 13
Eclipse / 14
Night of the Pigeons / 16
Tramroad / 17
Brightleaf / 18
Smoke / 20
Finishing Touches / 21
Back From the Funeral / 22
Homecoming / 23

Dragonfly

The Bed / 27
Monster / 28
How It's Come to This / 29
Ice / 30
What I'm Looking For / 31
Ember / 32
Basilisk / 33
Blood Moon / 34
Feral / 35
Sunday Morning / 36
The Question / 37
Educated Guess / 38
What You Still Wish For / 39

Dragonfly / 40
What I'll Settle For / 41

Meanwhile

Photographer's Paradiso / 45
Photographer's Inferno / 46
Horse Capital / 47
Sunday Clothes / 48
Figures of Speech / 49
Dog Days / 50
The Cloud I've Been Under / 53
Trigger / 54
The Tack / 55
Wilmington / 56
Last Call at Bethany Spring / 57
Seven Views of Owsley Fork / 59
Meanwhile / 60

Afterward

Afterward / 63
Rites of Spring / 64
Mea Culpa in Lexington Cemetery / 65
Daybook / 66
A Sonnet, Just in Case / 67
Death's Door / 68
The Bookcase / 69
Old Man / 72
The Blessing / 73
My Itinerary / 74
Tenancies / 75
A Visitation / 76
The Last Bur Oak at Mcconnell Springs / 77
Derby Day / 78
Early Evening, Late October / 79

Second Childhood / 80
Music / 81
When This Is All Over / 82

Notes / 85
Acknowledgments / 87
About the Author / 89

To the Blueberry Group,
which brought me back to poetry

It begins to snow in a country
Between the past and what I see,
Soft flakes like eyelids softly descending ...

— James Applewhite

HOMECOMING

FIRST LIGHT

Dew collects on the tobacco leaves,
dripping on the sandlugs
at the bottom of the stalks,
waking up the rattlesnakes.

Pecan trees sleepwalk in the orchard,
their branches splayed
like the arms of God
banishing the void with a wave.

In the house, a boy is dreaming
of his mother & father
standing in a field of tobacco,
growing smaller & smaller

as he leaves them behind.
He shifts in the sheets, wanting to weep
but not knowing why. The porch swing
swings at the slightest breeze.

GATHERING TOBACCO

Daddy makes me work right along with the hired hands in the field.
He gets big rough laughing boys from miles around to do the cropping.
They always know I'm the know-it-all dirt-farmer's kid—
booksmart but no common sense—who thinks he's above all this
but still has to work daylight to sundown all summer
just like they do, while his classmates in town sip Pepsi-Cola
by the pool. Daddy looks down from his seat on the tractor
& gives me a look. *Don't pay them no mind.*

It's chilly in the early mornings, dew like ice water
on the tobacco leaves. I dread touching the first leaf, always
dripping wet, & have to carry it with a sheaf of others under my arm,
which is why I've got on an undershirt & two outer shirts & a jacket,
layers I peel off one by one. When I snap the rubbery leaves off the stalk,
nasty green tobacco juice squirts out from the stems & sometimes
it catches me in the eye & burns. I'm soaked to the skin
with dew & sweat & pesticides when the sun comes out
& dries me off. Daddy waits till we throw our armfuls of leaves
on the trailer, then gives it the gas & creeps up the row.

By noon we're roasting, Daddy & the rough boys & me.
On sandlugging days early in the season, we bend down double
for the biggest & lowest leaves where the rattlesnakes nest
& a hot gust of our own stink drifts up from our collars & armpits.
Sometimes we go white in the face & throw up bile.
Daddy gives it the gas & yells *Load it or tote it, boys,*
& I feel small under the sky.

When the barn's full it's almost dark. Daddy pays the rough boys
in good hard cash, not a dime left over for me. I stand there
covered in black tobacco tar. He says *Don't know what I'd do*
without you, son. I don't know either & smile without showing my teeth
& wish he'd just go on & take the boys home so I can run to the house
& scrub myself all over with Ivory soap & drink a Pepsi-Cola.

JACOB'S LADDER

The packhouse bulging in early September,
my mother takes over, checking our work
as we strip the tobacco leaves off the sticks
they'd been lashed to & cured on,
each length of twine unstrung by hand
like pulling out stitches, each leaf laid
in a big cardboard mold like her springform
cake pan, the bundles stuffed into burlap sheets
tied off at the top like a hobo's sack.

On breaks over Sun Drop or Nehi Grape,
Mama uses loops of castoff twine
to teach us the old cat's-cradle tricks:
Crow's Feet, Cut Your Head Off, Fish in a Dish,
& my favorite, *Jacob's Ladder*—twelve
quick motions, ring-finger-middle-finger-thumb,
a flourish at the end & *there*—heaven's
spiral staircase, my hands on the banister,
at the top of it my inheritance.

UNDER THE HOOD

He was always there under the hood,
working on whatever piece-of-shit Ford or Dodge
we were stuck with that year. Peering at the dipstick,
splashing gasoline in the hacking carburetor,
fiddling with the hoses. The adjustable wrench
was always losing its grip, so his knuckles were skinned
& caked with blood, the bill of his baseball cap
smudged black with carbon dust. Muttered curses
streamed from his mouth like fumes threatening to ignite,
one eye shut against the smoke drifting up
from the cigarette clenched in his teeth,
the ash flaring orange with each breath in.
Who knew when this engine might throw a rod
& self-combust, or was it just a worn-out muffler,
blowing smoke? Either way, my mother & I stayed
out of reach. We knew firsthand what sparks could fly
if you connected the battery cables the wrong way
& what could boil over when the radiator got hot,
when you had to sit for a while & let it cool down
before you took off its cap.

MOUTHS TO FEED

My mama's people farmed sugar cane in South Carolina
& cut up stalks of it
for us to suck the sweetness from,
shucked their own oysters
& ground their own grits in the corncrib.
They wrung chickens' necks with their bare hands
for Sunday suppers,
slaughtered their own hogs & hung them upside down
from the branches of the pecan tree,
made their own sausages with black pepper & sage
& cured their own hams in the smokehouse.

My daddy's people farmed tobacco in North Carolina
& on putting-in days fed us & the farmhands
with gallons of stewed chicken bogged down in soupy rice
in a big black pot over an open fire
or with catfish fried in a cast-iron skillet,
the cornmeal crust crackling on your teeth.

My daddy lost money every year on the farm,
had to sell it off piece by piece
until he became a sharecropper on his own land.
Sometimes his sisters, who'd married well,
brought cans of creamed corn, bags of pinto beans,
a hambone,
& left them on the porch.
Other times he'd haul home blocks of government cheese
the size & shape of a loaf of light bread
& tell us not to say where it came from.

He'd drink black coffee at the kitchen table
late at night when everyone else had gone to bed,
cooling each sip in a saucer before he sipped it,
staring straight ahead.

THE NAPKINS

One of my fourth-grade English textbooks
included the tale of a little girl named Ellen
who went for dinner at a girlfriend's house
for the first time & saw to her horror that her friend's mother
had set the table with paper napkins instead of ones
made of cloth. At Ellen's own home, or so I pictured it
with the help of photographs I'd pored over
in the Sears catalog, breakfast & lunch were served
with neatly folded napkins made of absorbent cotton
& rolled into cylinders caught at the center
inside rings of wood or painted porcelain. At dinner
the napkins were linen, thicker than the best bedsheets
but just as soft, & folded into shapes like little tents
pitched atop the fine china. At the start of a meal,
her father would snap his napkin open with a flourish,
laying it gently across his lap.

Oh what a revelation it was to Ellen
that paper napkins existed, or that anyone she knew,
let alone a family at whose modest table she now
found herself dabbing her lips & fingers
with what felt like sandpaper, would use such things.
Oh how she pitied her poor classmate, resolving on the spot
to say nothing about it at home for fear that her parents
might forbid her ever to return. That night in bed,
or so I pictured it, she cried hot tears for her friend,
to whom she swore always to be kind.

At my own family's table that night,
I took notice for the first time that there were no napkins
of any description. There almost never were,
except for special occasions like the preacher dropping by
for fried chicken & deviled eggs after church. At best
we made do with a paper towel, or wiped our greasy fingers

on the same dishrag passed among us like a collection plate.
I shuddered to think what Ellen would have made of this,
but I knew. I knew.

Later in bed, I didn't cry for us
the way Ellen would've done. I told myself that at least
the plates were full & we bowed our heads & thanked the Lord
for the bounty we were about to receive before we dug into it
as if we were starving, as if it were our last meal on earth.

But, like Ellen, I said nothing to my parents about what I'd learned
that day in fourth grade, about how it clung to my hands
no matter how hard I wiped them on that dishrag,
how bitter it tasted on the tip of my tongue.

THE RIGHT TO REMAIN SILENT

My stomach rumbled like rolling thunder
that summer, full of beans and bacon
but still some hunger,
some odd appetite kept me up at night.

Hair sprouting like kudzu on my body,
I watched cop shows, one after another
with my mother,
who loved when the guilty were read their rights.

I worked in her seafood shop
that summer, dressing flats of fish—
their perfect flesh white,
their heads & guts tossed in a bucket of slop.

Under the covers with my flashlight,
I traded my comic books
for other subject matter
sneaked from my daddy's stash, & was sadder.

Nothing could wash the smell of the ocean off my hands
that summer, not even the girl I said I'd seduced
but never introduced
since she lived in the sea.

Anything I said could be used against me
in a court of law,
so I held my tongue.
I was young, after all, & not yet free

to say what I knew that summer
beyond a shadow of a doubt—
that I was not of this world nor it of me,
which left precious little to talk about.

VIRGINS

All of us virgins,
boys in the schoolyard swear by
our rubbers, size large.

ABECEDARIAN FOR ADOLESCENCE

A
boy
can
dream
every
fate,
get
help
if
jeers
kill
life's
mojo.
Night's
onanistic
promise:
queer
rhythms,
sleep,
those
unclean
visions.
Wait.
X-Acto
your
zit.

IT

In the dream the broomsedge field at sunset
is filled with boys playing hide & seek,
prowling the field not knowing who's It.

Each hides in the tall dry grass,
waiting to be found. Blond as the grass,
they ignore the candles coming on in the windows,

edge farther & farther toward the darkening woods.
Their clothes are torn, wisps of their hair
tangle in the briars. Hand over hand

they climb the trunks of trees, nest
in cradles of branches. Pale as possums,
their eyes flash pink in the light

of the huge moon rising. Their voices
grow deep as they bay to each other, over
& over, *Find me. Find me. Find me.*

ECLIPSE

You view a solar eclipse
which they say you shouldn't look directly at
because it will damage your eyes
& maybe your brain for the rest of your life
but you can't resist
& stand in the yard at the appointed time
& sure enough the moon passes in front of the sun
which goes black with a rim of white like a dilated eye
& you look at everything all around you
& it seems that night has fallen in an instant

& it occurs to you that this is the real world,
this, & that all those bright shining days
you thought you had passed through
were in fact a twilight at best & more often
akin to midnight, that the sun itself
is an illusion, the world itself an illusion
to shield you from the truth
that this is not your home.

But in the next moment everything looks normal,
the farmhouse with its small rooms
& peeling paint, the mimosa tree in the dusty yard,
the tobacco field across the dirt road
shimmering in midday heat, your parents blinking
& squinting & asking what's wrong with you
& your brother rolling his eyes & laughing.

That very night you stand on the porch
with its crumbling floorboards & creaking swing
& study the pockmarked moon
where two men will soon be walking
with its rocks & craters & dust & gravity so minimal
it barely keeps you from floating away,
& you picture what will happen next

as you leap off the porch into the black & twinkling sky
& keep on going, up to the moon
with its pale gleaming face & its sea of tranquility
& its other side in perpetual shadow
with all those hiding places
& beyond it the stars—

NIGHT OF THE PIGEONS

In the dream our mothers protest
at first, but rumors of a plague
convince them our fathers are right.

Before dawn in the square
near the general's statue, we spread
millet & seeds laced with poison.

At sunrise, from their roosts
in the eaves, the pigeons come.
All day we watch them feed & die.

At dusk we lay a bonfire
& work hour by hour,
pitching the pigeons one by one

on the flames, filling the sky
with smoke. I lay down with the boys
& wake at midnight, one last bird

still in my hand, throat-feathers
phosphor blue & dancing in the light.
I fling it on the fire—

from which it lifts, cooing my name
as it flashes past my ear,
rustling its ashen wings.

TRAMROAD

They logged these pinewoods
before I was born, built a tram
to haul the lumber out. Now what's left
is this tramroad, the forest erasing it
year by year, saplings in the median,

taking it all back. They took up the tracks
for scrap metal years ago, but stray spikes
& railroad ties still hide in the trestle beds
or under pine straw, everything returning
to where it came from.

I'm a teenage boy on a Christmas errand,
an axe in my hand. No Douglas firs here
but some nice Eastern whites, their needles
firm & fragrant, perfect for ornaments
& garlands, & years from now

I'll wonder how far I had to walk down this road
before it disappeared altogether,
before the pines towered & swayed
in that sweet clean breeze without a trace
of smoke, before they stopped me & beat me back,

before I spotted my little tree shivering
at the foot of the old mill's sawdust pile,
before I chopped it down & dragged it away,
before it fell to me & my eye for such things
to dress it with tinsel & lights & a star.

BRIGHTLEAF

I watch you lean on a fencepost at sunset
& light up a Marlboro—
the slow deep drag you hold in your lungs
as long as you can, swelling your chest
with tar & ashes & the greatest solace
you've ever known.

You grow the stuff, a fourth-generation master
of curing the green tobacco leaves of July & August
to the color of the burlap sacks
we haul them off to market in
come September.

Sometimes you hold a tobacco leaf
to your nose, inhale its dark bouquet
like a snifter of brandy.

You don't let the word *cancer* be spoken in our house.
When by chance I'm the one to tell you
that your best friend died of it,
I see you cry for the first time
& the last.

At the fence you know I'm watching from the porch,
know I'll run from this farm as soon as I can,
know there'll be no fifth generation,
know it ends with you.

I watch you fire up another cigarette
& pull on it hard, its tip flaring in the fading light,
& your face, cured half a century
in the smoke of two packs a day,
is revealed as your finest brightleaf,
veined, tanned, supple, creased,
a parchment treasure map that in my mind

I fold and re-fold till it's soft as linen,
ready to memorize & burn.

SMOKE

It gets in your eyes.

It rises from the ashes
you scatter on your clothes,
a mist that lifts from the swamp
& climbs the steps to your bedroom
in the middle of the night,
sits on your chest & steals your breath like a cat.

It's neighborly, settling
on the porches of your heart & lungs
& setting a spell.

It issues from your mouth as a skein of silk
like a magic trick, a ghost tongue
uncoiling like a dancing snake.

It sighs like the soul leaving the body at death.

It circles your head like a wreath.

FINISHING TOUCHES

Holding a hand for the last time,
your fingers linger on a wrinkle,
a lifeline you'll never touch again,
& you tell yourself that maybe memory
is enough, just enough, if it lasts.

Perhaps it will last, but it won't be enough.
Tomorrow, oh, & years from now
it won't be this still warm palm,
this hand that took your trembling hand
& held it, all that night, till morning.

BACK FROM THE FUNERAL

Daddy's dead but the wash is still wet,
so Mama & I stand side by side
at the strand of fence wire strung between the pecan trees
in the orchard late this breezy afternoon,
her mouth full of clothespins
so no word between us, no sound at all
but our breathing in, breathing out,
& I hand her my cloroxed T-shirts to hang on the line,
the wind filling their sleeves as if with shoulders,
our own shoulders touching,
our own arms splayed like the limbs of these trees
that have sheltered us all our lives,
holding off the setting sun.

HOMECOMING

Flashing past in my rented car,
tobacco rows buckling in the corner of my eye,
each mile east from Raleigh/Durham
pumps me full of upper & downer.
Power windows rolled up, I keep the radio
on jazz & NPR, though at eight years old
I wore out a Kitty Wells album—
You don't have to tell me things I already knew,
every time your lips would lie, your eyes would tell on you—
& in silence watch the world become
the one I came from: the vast
immaculate greens of Fort Bragg,
the Lumber River spillway, Boardman's
knife-fight dancehall, Cow Branch
rippling with water moccasins,
breadbox trailer homes
parked in front of the boarded-up shacks people were born in
& can't bring themselves to tear down.

The Southern Railway still chugs by
hauling God knows what, still blowing the distant whistle
that had me running toward the train
when I heard it as a boy,
hoping for a ride.

The house is gone, all but the chimney
on the farm's last quarter-acre.
The old Dodge pickup sits stranded on cinder blocks
in the shade of the chinaberry tree.
The tobacco barn's choked with vines
like Sleeping Beauty's castle.
Daddy's tractor's parked forever.

The pecan trees shed their leaves
like the ashes from his cigarette,
covering my feet.

DRAGONFLY

THE BED

At first it feels so small
    like a full-size bed
or even a twin, the two of you

smashed together, his body
    draped around yours
or yours around his

like a duvet filled with
    the feathers of each other's
breathing, no room

& no need for another
    square inch of space
between you. Then winter

turns to spring & summer
    & all either of you can stand
is a thin cotton sheet

barely touching the skin
    in this sweltering room
& you move away from each other

as the bed swells to king-size
    at least, a vast
& all but impassable continent.

By late autumn it's cold again
    & the bed has grown enormous
as the world & you're in it

alone, frozen in place
    on the same side as always,
shivering.

MONSTER

The monster crawls up
from under the bed & climbs
inside my mirror.

HOW IT'S COME TO THIS

1
I liked to watch you
sleep, your face soft, breathing through
your delicate mouth.

2
I took your portrait
& you refused to smile. I
came to know that look.

3
Right before you leave
is when it's worst, when I see
you're already gone.

4
Sometimes I wonder
how it's come to this, & then
I remember how.

5
I'm a teen again,
drifting off to old love songs
on the radio.

6
Sometimes you're still here
in the dark, breathing in my
ear. I reach for you—

ICE

There must be a way
to stop the wanting,
to pack my heart in ice
like pricey steaks
sent through the mail

so I can look you
in the eye & say
I don't want you anymore
& believe
that every word is true.

WHAT I'M LOOKING FOR

The cypresses on the limestone ramparts
        of Ellington Parkway, silent sentries
    at roadside memorials as I drive by, my headlights strafing
           makeshift crosses, tattered garlands—

and it's late, & later, & the later it gets
        the more I need Coltrane & Hartman
    caressing Strayhorn—*Then you came along*
          with your siren song, to tempt me to madness—

& now around midnight the asphalt's wet, & wetter,
        floodlit signs from the all-night joints
    on Dickerson Road reflected in flooded gutters,
          rippling like ribbons in the wind:

Club Mirage, Private Dancer, the Congress Inn,
        & the Love Doctor with her blood-red neon palm
    beckoning in the window—*I thought for a while*
        that your poignant smile

was tinged with a sadness of a great love for me—
        ah, yes, I was wrong … again … & the women & men
    standing under street lamps in pools of light
        turning their eyes as I pass in my car,

straining to see what I'm looking for—
        but what I'm looking for is down this street
    I can't see the end of, in a smoky bar
        where you still sit, smiling back.

EMBER

for Kimberly Miller

In the cooling hearth

          I caught you once

an ember in the ashes

          looking at me

found some new fuel

          from the corner of your eye

& burst into flame

          for one long moment

till it lapsed like a lamp

          as if to spy on me

out of oil

          when I didn't know

& a coil of smoke

          I was being watched

rose up & danced

          as if you were thinking of

a snake being charmed

          taking me back

BASILISK

After he broke my little finger, snapping the bone to make me let go of my phone, it swelled by half & the ligament pulled tight, leaving the finger curved inward like a claw. The middle knuckle froze, useless for typing. Gloves were out of the question. No health insurance then so I didn't get it fixed. For years I kept my left hand balled into a fist, hoping that no one would notice the claw, the knuckle turned to stone. When anyone did, I'd tell a story about being jumped by a stranger on a street one night. No one questioned it. I even bragged that I had put up a struggle & held onto the phone, as if I'd been brave. This week I tell the story to the therapist working on my finger, stretching the ligament, prying it open. The knuckle is still frozen but she's determined. She dips my hand in hot paraffin, pulls off the glove of wax & stretches my finger, presses it down with heavy weights. It hurts, almost as much as it did that night, but she holds my hand as she does it, the first time anyone has held it since he did. I want to tell her that he wasn't a stranger, that it wasn't on the street, that he'd held my hand other times, too, & it never hurt except that once. I want to tell her who he was, but that would be telling her who I was then. Instead I ask if she's ever heard of a basilisk, an ancient monster that looks at its prey & turns it into stone. A basilisk looked at my hand, I tell her, & see what happened? She says at least it was just a finger.

BLOOD MOON

You kick him out but not all the way out,
always insisting you want peace & quiet
but in your heart it's the last thing you want
or ever wanted. What's it all been for,
if not the way the hair on the back of your neck
stands up when he looks at you? Sometimes
you want him gone forever with his howling lying
beautiful mouth & you don't give a damn
how empty you are without him. But then
things slow way down & get way too quiet
& instead of thinking about him every second
of your life, you start thinking about yourself
& there's a reason why you stay away from mirrors.
It's just easier in the end to have him there with his
lip curled & his fist balled because then you know
who you are. Plus there's a blood moon tonight
& what a waste it would be without him looming
in your bedroom door, claws out & hackles up
& in his yellow eyes that same old look.

FERAL

Just don't let them know
how feral you really are,
how little you care.

SUNDAY MORNING

I watch the waiter bring your usual order, a mound of chicken salad on a bed of lettuce, to your table on the sidewalk. It has sliced grapes in it, I think, maybe some walnuts. Your new boyfriend is having quiche Lorraine, one of my favorites back then. You look good, your teeth flashing white when you smile. There's a silver pitcher of cream for the coffee, a bowl of sugar. A basket of croissants, a saucer with pats of butter, & a single flower, a yellow dahlia, in a tiny vase. You don't see me because I'm standing in the shadows in the alley across the street, & because you keep your eyes on him. Even if you glanced in my direction, you might not recognize me. It's hypothetical, though, because I refuse to say a word to you, a single word that would ruin your perfect breakfast on this perfect Sunday morning. So I wait in the alley, watch you chew & swallow & sip & smile at him, watch him smile back, watch the two of you rise & walk off down the street, holding hands, until you're far enough away. Then I run across the street to your table & scoop up what's left of the chicken salad in a paper sack. I set off in the opposite direction with the busboy's eyes on my back, walking fast, almost running, crushing the dahlia in my fist.

THE QUESTION

Sometimes you just live with what happened,
let it lie asleep on the rug at your feet,
since after all it will wake one day
from the dream it's been dreaming
& raise its head to look you in the face
& ask the very question you've been dreading,
to which you wish you had no answer
but you do.

EDUCATED GUESS

He was two blocks in front of me when I spotted him. I couldn't see his face, but something about the way he walked made me think he was someone I knew, & it seemed important that I should catch up to him & have a friendly conversation, which seems to happen so rarely these days. I quickened my pace, almost running, but when I had reduced the distance between us to a single block, a car turned in front of me & cut me off, & then there was more traffic, so I had to wait as I watched him receding in the distance, leaving me behind all over again. When at last I was able to make it through the crosswalk, starting to run this time, he turned onto a side street & I couldn't see him anymore. I broke into a sprint, rounded the corner & there he was, gazing into a store window, absorbed by the sight of two mannequins, both male, standing close to each other & wearing beautiful clothes not unlike his own, & I nearly bumped into him. He looked at me then, surprised & a little fearful but not unkind, & I understood how I must have appeared, dressed in my usual fashion, breathing hard, perspiring freely, perhaps in the early stages of some medical emergency or psychotic episode, & I could see that he was not anyone I knew or would ever know. Yet after a moment he seemed to know me, or to be able to make an educated guess about me, & he asked whether I was all right, if he could help me in any way, & I said no, just no, answering both questions at once.

WHAT YOU STILL WISH FOR

Even though it always burns you
like an ember in the ashes
you thought had gone cold.

Even though the last time around
is like a fishbone in your throat
you can't choke down.

Even though you know perfectly well
it will make you wish you were never born
all over again.

Even though you swear on your life
it's the last thing on your mind,
the very last thing.

DRAGONFLY

I want what you have.
      I want to see what you see
            with your flickering, prismatic eyes

skimming the river in flood
      between us, surveying the damage,
            letting it lie. I want your long limbs

like oars, your tail a rudder in the wind
      as you sail away downstream toward the sea.
            Most of all, oh most of all

I want your translucent, tessellated wings,
      the light beneath them lavender
            as if passing through windows in churches.

Don't leave me standing here
      on the far shore waving. Take me
            with you. Come back. Come back.

WHAT I'LL SETTLE FOR

The list grows longer every year.
Instead of hardwood I accept an old rug
even though it's frayed, an easy chair
that fits my bones if not the room.

In place of a crackling fire & a hearth,
my little space heater taking the chill
off the bathroom tiles, keeping me company
as I soak & doze in the narrow tub.

On chilly mornings, the silhouettes
of leaves dancing on venetian blinds
as I take in the show from my bed,
alone beneath the faded coverlet.

My hand-thrown earthen coffee mug
rough & ridged from the potter's fingers,
the hand that held it holding my hand,
the flame that kissed it kissing my lips.

MEANWHILE

PHOTOGRAPHER'S PARADISO

It's always
early morning or late
afternoon, the light

crisp as a glass
of cold Chardonnay,
or else the blue

hour, the moon
a slice of orange
in a sangria sky

as a stranger waits
till you're ready
before busting a move

on the street,
his face drunk
with joy, his head

flung back
at just the right angle
for you to click

the shutter & capture
for eternity
one perfect day.

PHOTOGRAPHER'S INFERNO

It's always that morning leaving New Orleans on I-10
when you see in the corner of your eye a small boat
in the bayou to your right, a breeze ruffling the surface
of the shining water & a seated fisherman casting his line
in a perfect arc across the narrow channel toward a stand
of swaying sweetgrass. You start to salivate & begin
to pull over with your camera ready in the passenger's seat
but an eighteen-wheeler's right on your ass & you hesitate,
just a second, & the next second you've missed your chance,
that rippling carpet of diamonds & a thin strand of nylon
catching the light & defining the line between water & sky
lost in an instant. You drive on toward Biloxi, your mouth
brackish with the brine of an image that will stay with you
as long as you live, a picture that no one but you will ever see.

HORSE CAPITAL

Sad to live in the Horse Capital of the World
& have nothing to do with horses.

It makes you feel left out,
prone to pretend you know who Oliver Lewis was
& why it's called bluegrass
when the grass clearly isn't blue

& why, on those cold misty mornings
when you can see the colts' breath
as they gambol in the pasture on your right
as you drive downtown to your office,
you wonder what would happen
if you were that colt on your third birthday
with thousands of people watching
as you stand trembling at the gate,
ready to run.

SUNDAY CLOTHES

Lovely Lexington
in Sunday clothes, Saturday's
bourbon on her breath.

FIGURES OF SPEECH

I try to do unto others
as I would have them do unto me,
though I find this awfully hard at times,
especially when those others
have already done unto me
that which I would never have done unto them,
in which case I might be sorely tempted
to do unto them
that which they did unto me, since after all,
they did it first.

If I don't have anything good to say
I try very hard to say nothing at all,
but a word or two do slip out now & then,
which tends to get back
to the person I had nothing good to say about
but spoke of anyway,
at which point that person often has a word or two
to say right back,
none of it very good, to be perfectly honest,
& then we have ourselves a conversation.

I like to say *Bless your heart*,
& I do mean it with all my heart,
but in my heart of hearts I mean it in different ways,
depending,
since as we all know, the heart wants what it wants
& sometimes it has no clue what it wants
but it sure does want it, at least mine does,
& sometimes what it wants
is to bless your heart, other times not to bless it,
not to bless it one blessèd bit.

DOG DAYS

[In the dog days of summer] the Sea boiled, the Wine turned sour, Dogs grew mad … and all other creatures became languid; causing to man, among other diseases, burning fevers, hysterics, and phrensies.

      —*Clavis Calendria*, or, *A Compendious Analysis of the Calendar* by John Brady, 1813

The phrase is actually a reference to the fact that, during this time, the Sun occupies the same region of the sky as Sirius, the brightest star visible from any part of Earth and part of the constellation Canis Major, the Greater Dog.

      —*The Farmer's Almanac*, 2019

Remember that time when my old aunt Almira Gulch
took her morning constitutional with that umbrella of hers
& got bit on the ankle by that mutt from the farm across the field,

the one they called Toto? Aunt Almira set out on her bicycle
to take that beast to the sheriff's to receive the wages of sin,
as was fitting & proper given the grievous harm visited upon her person,

but the little girl cried, & *her* old aunt rubbed salt in the wound
by informing Aunt Almira that she'd waited all those years
to tell her what she thought of her but now,

being a so-called Christian woman, she couldn't *say* it!
But when my aunt got to the sheriff's, Toto was gone,
having escaped right out of her basket, thereby cheating Aunt Almira

of her righteous retribution & postponing the eternal damnation
which was that dog's rightful due in the eyes of the Lord.
And that's when it *hit* the fan!

First of all, the sheriff wouldn't do a G.D. thing.
He just sat there like a bump on a log, fanning himself
& sipping what he *claimed* was ice tea—

Aunt Almira always swore she smelled Mogen David on his breath,
which might explain why he didn't even rise to his feet
when a lady entered the room—

although between me & you, it *was* mighty hot
that time of year, the middle of August, hot enough to fry an egg
on her bicycle seat, which we all know she kept warmed up year round—

& with all *due* respect for Aunt Almira,
I always did wonder just how she could possibly have known
what Mad Dog smelled like, bless her heart—

but the sheriff had bigger eggs to fry,
what with the cyclone that hit that same afternoon,
after which I expect he helped himself to *another* glass of tea.

None of that stopped her, of course, from pitching a fit.
I tell you what, she threw the book at that man,
starting with *an eye for an eye, a tooth for a tooth,*

moving on to Revelations—*For without are dogs,*
& sorcerers, & whoremongers, & murderers, & idolaters—
& finishing up with Sodom & Gomorrah

which I think she threw in for good measure
since it *was* her all-time favorite—then flounced out in a huff,
hopped on her bike & *flew* back home.

After the storm blew over, I made the mistake
of knocking on Aunt Almira's door to check on her,
only to find her carrying on something terrible.

She said she'd fallen asleep, it being so hot & all,
& had a nightmare of a house falling from the sky,
right on top of her twin sister Alvira—

& that little girl & her canine abomination
just *prancing* down some old brick road
with a scarecrow & a lion & a pansy with an axe,

51

ever last one of them going *straight* to hell.
That night I slipped a nip of Mad Dog in her glass of ice tea
& put her to bed. I thought maybe Toto'd given her rabies—

for weeks she kept getting up at midnight in her sweaty nightgown,
looking for the brightest star in the sky & muttering
I'll get you, my pretty, & your little dog, too!

But the bite on her ankle healed up fine,
& by the time the weather turned cooler in September
my old Aunt Almira was back in the saddle,

burning up the road & laying *down* the law.
But for the rest of her days she kept well clear of that dog
on the farm across the field, & ever time the wind picked up

& tumbleweeds came rolling down the path
she made a beeline for the storm cellar, peeking out now & then
for anything falling from the sky.

THE CLOUD I'VE BEEN UNDER

It's when I plant my feet
that the street beneath me
starts to shift.
It's when I laugh out loud
that the cloud I've been under
starts to lift.

It's when I'm feeling old
that I'm told I'm returning
to my youth.
It's when I start to cry
that the lie I've been telling
is the truth.

TRIGGER

A trigger warning:
You are reading poetry.
It'll be okay.

THE TACK

Sink or swim
with her or him,

black or white
or dark or light,

look high & low
in rain or snow

for this or that,
tit for tat.

Space & time,
rhythm, rhyme,

all these so dear
I'd like to hear

them every day,
if I may.

Let it be,
set it free,

make a sound
that goes around

the world & back.
Take the tack

that life's a treat
if there's a beat

& it swings.
Strum those strings.

WILMINGTON

for Joe Anthony

I spent my childhood thirty miles inland,
watching *The Jim Burns Show* on the NBC
affiliate & reading the *Morning Star*. I see it
like an old black & white movie—we'd cruise
down Ocean Boulevard to Wrightsville Beach,
tour the old battleship *USS North Carolina*
docked forever in the Cape Fear River,
eat fried shrimp at Calabash. It was an easy,
airy, sea-salted city. Mini-golf in the sun. Azaleas
in the shade. Driveways paved with crushed oyster shells.

Never once did I hear a single word
about what happened on November 10, 1898,
when Alfred Moore Waddell & a mob of white
supremacists armed with rifles & a Gatling gun
burned the black *Daily Record* to the ground
& then went house to house, slaughtering at least
sixty black people & up to three hundred, then staged
a *coup d'état*, replacing the biracial city council
& installing their own mayor, Waddell, who'd vowed
never to surrender *to a ragged raffle of Negroes,*
even if we have to choke the Cape Fear River with carcasses.

I'm sixty when I learn about the Tulsa massacre
from a superhero miniseries on HBO. I'm sixty-one,
standing in the driveway in Lexington
with my New Jersey-born landlord, when he tells me
what happened in Wilmington, his voice rising in anger
& falling in sorrow, & the black & white movie
of my youth starts to play again, this time in color.

LAST CALL AT BETHANY SPRING

for Libby Falk Jones & Br. Paul Quenon

(Bethany Spring Retreat Center,
New Haven, Kentucky, 2019)

We sit in circles
& ponder the significance of birds,
the red-tailed hawk riding the sky above the old farmhouse,
the bobwhites with their healing two-tone call

that Brother Paul now hears so rarely,
the sunset a great firebird spreading its scarlet wings
across the west horizon in early evening,
reflected in the dregs of the drained lake.

We're the last band of seekers in this place,
the house sold off to the distillery next door as a bed & breakfast
with no meditation room, no portraits of Jesus or Merton or Buddha.
The air's at once thin as a veil between worlds

yet thick with benediction
as we embrace our fate as punctuating spirits
completing a circle, the last in a line of poets & pilgrims
that goes back half a century.

Some of us are young, sprinting down the shaded lane
or giggling with our Berea classmates late at night,
while one of us wonders if this hobble upstairs to bed on a bad knee
might be his last in this world.

Still there's time to consider the meaning of trees—
from the benefits of *shinrin-yoku*, forest bathing,
to the silver poplar shedding its nightgown in the yard,
& down the road this autumn afternoon

the great sycamore at the Abbey of Gethsemani,
its naked torso the color of bones, its outstretched arms

sheltering us as we lie on the dying grass,
its fingertips testing the wind.

Back at the house, we attune ourselves to the quiet.
Sounds that might have been lost in the cities we came from
reach us here: the distant cock crow
announcing one more morning,

the low toll of the Vespers bell
that rolls down the hill & lodges in our spines,
& the long high chime with which we close our final circle,
reverberating in the thin space between this world & the next.

SEVEN VIEWS OF OWSLEY FORK

for Linda Bryant & Coleman Davis

1
Fog rolls down Big Hill.
A boat on the reservoir
vanishes in mist.

2
Hepatica, wild
orchids, trout lilies, this day,
all ephemeral.

3
The wind in the trees
makes the sound of a rainstorm,
a rushing river.

4
Three buzzards circle
high in the sky, nonchalant,
taking in the sights.

5
Afternoon shadows
stretch across the lake toward me,
their arms beckoning.

6
The sun sinks behind
the ridge. Oh let me lie down
in all that stardust.

7
In the bright morning
a flock of geese flies over,
honking, coming home.

MEANWHILE

These are the lives we've been given,
all these bright shining mornings
& dark starless nights, all these damned & beloved children
lost & found & found & lost,
all these tears.

Of course there's no changing the past
no matter what color glasses
we look at it through, nor is there any confusion
about where we're headed, only how we'll get there
& when.

Till then, the world is harsh & cold
but for what we bring to it in our little rooms,
the cups of coffee we pour each other
& warm our hands with, the cream & the sugar,
the barely burnt crusts of bread.

AFTERWARD

AFTERWARD

With no one to call them, the animals in the garden
forget their names. Their truce, too:
in sudden hunger they hunt each other,
rending the air with screams of the kill.

In garden paths once worn smooth
by the tread of soft bare feet,
grass grows, then saplings, erasing
every trace of man or woman or god.

Where once there were only spring & summer,
now comes autumn, the shimmering tree
at the edge of the garden so heavy with fruit
that its branches bow down to the ground.

With no one to pick them, the ripened apples
fall from the tree, luscious in the light,
& are eaten by birds who scatter their seed
in fertile fields far from the garden.

High in the tree, two eyes watch.
A mouth shoots out an exploratory tongue,
tastes winter on the wind, & begins to invent
an alphabet, starting with the letter *S*.

RITES OF SPRING

The neighborhood tabby & her annual litter
scamper out of sight like ghosts in pilfered slippers.
Bees are sheathed like fingers in the foxgloves.
Young ferns unfurl their curved stems like tongues.

At the foot of a pear tree, mama cat skulks,
stalking a carefree squirrel who dares her to pounce.
She calls his bluff with a thud, then flounces home
with jaws full of supper, trailing drops of blood.

MEA CULPA IN LEXINGTON CEMETERY

Two & a half centuries have scrubbed your names
off the oldest gravestones the way streams rub pebbles
smooth in a riverbed. Elsewhere moss & lichen

cover the engraved words like shrouds. Sometimes
you're obscured where your crosses & obelisks
have been tilted by the roots of a sycamore pressing up

through your bones. Here & there the willows bend
low enough to touch you with their many hands,
their fingertips straining to decipher the fading braille

of your epitaphs—*Beloved Husband, Devoted Wife.*
No one else gets half as near, least of all the groundskeepers
who know a losing battle when they see one. Your people

& their people & their people lie beside you now,
their names still legible though give it time. Turns out
even limestone is no match for the lathe of eternity. Ah

well. Accept this apology, please, & console yourself.
Remember how beautiful you were at the end, your eyes
flickering like the candles burning down by your beds?

So too these stone headboards at whose feet you sleep
so soundly, fine antiques still acquiring their high patina
by the hour & the day & the year.

DAYBOOK

2020

1
Streets almost empty.
Late at night they haunt me now,
those wailing sirens.

2
For twenty-four hours
I think I've got it. Write my
will & testament.

3
After lunch I just
say *fuck it* & lie facedown
on the hardwood floor.

4
Of all things to be
reassured by: lawnmowers,
the smell of cut grass.

5
We get accustomed
to everything soon enough,
even all these dead.

6
The solace of ice
in a glass, lime, gin, tonic,
bitter as the nights.

7
This rainy morning
I watch you turn a corner
& like that, you're gone.

A SONNET, JUST IN CASE

2020

I know I'm not supposed to write these lines
about this virus, not just yet. Too soon,
too soon. They say to wait like grapes on vines
for one more season, one more harvest moon—
but darling, what if there's an early frost?
I'll never have this chance to tell you how
I loved our time together. Nothing's lost
when written down this quickly, even now.
So please forgive my haste to set in stone
how beautiful you were, that day we met,
how much more beautiful you've grown
each day & night since then. We're not done yet.
But if you wake to find me getting gone,
you'll have these words I left you, moving on.

DEATH'S DOOR

You can't miss it.
It's the last house on the block,
a bit run down but lots of curb appeal—
a widow's walk on the mansard roof,
a weather vane that always points south,
tall beveled windows with the shutters closed
day & night.

The owner's been there forever.
A gentleman who mostly keeps to himself,
he takes long walks of an evening
with his collar turned up, his fedora pulled low.
Sometimes he'll nod when you pass him on the sidewalk.
Sometimes from across the street
he'll wave.

You take it as an invitation
& one day soon or years from now
you'll find yourself standing at his door,
admiring the old brass doorknob rubbed to a shine.
Put your good eye to the keyhole,
see nothing but darkness,
knock.

THE BOOKCASE

I came across *Two Years Before the Mast*,
a memoir by Richard Henry Dana, Jr.,
published by Harper & Brothers in 1840
in the bookcase in our house in 1970, when I was ten,
part of a set of the Harvard Classics,
selected by Harvard President Charles W. Eliot
& first published by P.F. Collier & Son in 1909 & 1910
as *Dr. Eliot's Five Foot Shelf of Books.*
I didn't read it then—I wasn't sure what a mast was,
though perhaps it had to do with ships—
but I did read some of the other books on the shelves
including *Little Women* by Louisa May Alcott,
published in two volumes in 1868 & 1869,
which I knew from the title was a girl's story
but read even so, in the privacy of my room,
& which became the first of many books
to make me cry, the death of sweet, kind Beth—
Every day I lose a little, & feel more sure
that I shall never gain it back. It's like the tide, Jo,
when it turns; it goes slowly, but it can't be stopped—
too much for my young heart.

I didn't tell anyone about my tears, not my parents
& certainly not my older brother, who never read books
but spent most of his time in the woods, hunting.
One cold morning in deer season
he put a shotgun loaded with buckshot shells in my hands
& commanded me to fire it,
to *be a man* for once in my life,
but I was terrified of what would have been
the deafening blast, the stink of gunsmoke,
the kick of the stock against my shoulder
& of what it was all for, killing things
for fun, & of the thought that if I pulled the trigger

I would be the buckshot, exchanging my world for his,
a world of smoke & fire & blood,
a world without books.

Half a century later, on one of the last days
of the pandemic year of 2020,
I downloaded *Two Years Before the Mast*,
whose author's studies at Harvard, of all places,
were interrupted in 1834 by a case of measles
that left his eyes too weak to read
& so he went to sea as a common sailor
on a merchant brig called the *Pilgrim*,
which sailed south from Boston Harbor, circling Argentina
en route to California—an undertaking
calculated to kill or cure, as Dr. Eliot put it,
& which accomplished the latter, luckily,
& taught him, along the way,
how not to be a man.

Dana wrote of watching the ship commander, a Captain Thompson,
flog a sailor named Sam he'd set his mind against,
whipping his naked back with a heavy rope.
Then another sailor who was his close friend, a Swede named John
who dared ask why Sam was being flogged,
was himself flogged. *"No," shouted the captain; "nobody
shall open his mouth aboard this vessel, but myself;"
and began laying the blows upon his back,
swinging half round between each blow, to give it
full effect. As he went on, his passion increased,
& he danced about the deck, calling out as he swung the rope—
"If you want to know what I flog you for, I'll tell you.
It's because I like to do it!—because
I like to do it!"*

In 1976, when he was still a teenager,
my brother was cited for nightshining,
an illegal hunting technique
in which he used the headlights of our pickup truck
to blind deer at night, freeze them in their tracks
& shoot them where they stood, grazing at the edge of the woods.
Half a century later, in 2016, a few weeks after proudly
announcing that he'd voted for Donald Trump,
he died alone of cardiac arrest, his house
full of shotguns & buckshot & almost no books,
the copies of *Two Years Before the Mast* and *Little Women*
—the latter of which I'd recalled as part of the Harvard Classics
but was wrong, Dr. Eliot having excluded novels
& work in all genres written by women
except for the occasional poet—
long gone.

As I was beginning to write this poem in early 2021
with the coronavirus ravaging the world,
I did some reading about Alcott
& learned that the character of Beth in *Little Women*
was based on the author's beloved sister Lizzie,
who died in the aftermath of a different contagion,
scarlet fever, in 1858 at the age of twenty-two,
not sweetly & quietly like Beth
but in fury, her body ravaged by the disease,
driven mad by pain so terrible that heavy doses of opium
had no effect, & she raged at her fate
& commanded her sisters to leave her alone,
although just before the end she seemed to let go
& her last words that they could understand were
*Well now, mother, I go, I go. How beautiful
everything is tonight.*

OLD MAN

Turn up your collar,
old man. The night is so cold,
home so far away.

THE BLESSING

2020

With the news so uniformly depressing
I retreat to my kitchen
& make some pinto beans with a little bacon
& some fresh-baked cornbread
to sop up the juice,

& sit down to eat
with the ghost of my old Aunt Addie at my elbow
clinking the ice cubes
in her glass of sweet tea,
waiting for me to ask the blessing.

MY ITINERARY

2021

I take long walks at night
& find that I can see the whole world clearly,
the stars & everything under the stars, all of it
twinkling & shining.

I stroll in the cemetery
& learn that my imaginary friends never left me
as I'd been thinking so bitterly, that in fact
they've been tagging along in silence
all this time.

I cross into the underworld
& chat with Hades & Persephone,
who are sharing a pomegranate.
They offer me some seeds
which I gobble down, losing track entirely
of how many.

TENANCIES

for Laverne Zabielski & Larry Vogt

Sometimes I think I hear them, the ones who lived here
before me. The old man found dead in the bedroom
two days after his only friend last heard from him,
the apartment swaddled in cat hair. The young man
who died of AIDS & whose mother planted yellow roses
in his memory that bloom by my front steps each spring,
gone by early summer. The old friend who sheltered here
after her divorce, then welcomed her ex-husband so often
that she remembered why she loved him. The single moms
whose rowdy kids trashed the place, the single dads
who drank & chain-smoked every night, coating the walls
with soot. The old man snoring as his naps get longer
& longer, the young man pacing the hallway & sleeping
less & less, the old friend sighing as her gentleman caller
touches her in all the old places in a whole new way
& she marries him again. Decades after their forwarding
addresses have expired, I still get their mail. *Return
to sender*, I scrawl. *No longer at this address*. Truth is
we're all here together, roommates for life & then some,
keeping each other company.

A VISITATION

1
I wake to the scent
of grandma's lilac hand cream
wafting in the air.

2
Do the dead return?
If not, whose fingers are these
pulling at my sleeve?

3
The aroma shifts
to lard, buttermilk, her hands
moving in the flour.

4
Hot from the oven,
her biscuits are ridged on top
where she pressed them down.

5
Her apron comes loose
at the back & she lets me
tie the strings again.

6
In bed I can smell
Beechnut snuff, Doublemint gum,
both sweet on her breath.

THE LAST BUR OAK AT MCCONNELL SPRINGS

They don't know exactly how old you are
because your massive chest is mostly hollow—
Too many voids, the forester says, *too few rings
to count inside*—but you're pushing three hundred
& look every day of it. You stood here before
Lexington was Lexington, before the old mill,
before these twenty-six acres encircled by the city
were saved as a woodland park in the nineties.
Your long limbs stretch across the trail
with the help of crutches now, tall stiff poles
to rest your arms on so you won't tip over in a storm
like your brother did a few years back. I figure
you're lonely, the last of your kind. Some afternoons
I keep you company, resting on the bench at your feet,
shooting the breeze. I tell you that I lost my brother
too, that my heart's as full of voids, that my joints
are just as creaky when the nights get cold.
Who can say which of us will be the last one
standing? I hope it's you.

DERBY DAY

In other years I might have been
at Churchill Downs, screaming in the infield
with the rest of the slobs, tearing up betting slips
as most of my picks come in dead last
& doing my best not to think about the horses
who didn't make it to the gate—fractured femur,
broken down. This year I'm broken down myself,
one way or another. Too close to the bone.

Folks in Kentucky say it's safe to plant a garden
after Derby Day, so I scatter a handful of seeds
from a friend in a bucket of soil on the porch.
I water the soft dark dirt, pat it down,
planting & burying the same motion of the hands.
Police horses clip-clop by on the street.
Lincoln's cortège must've sounded like this.

Night's coming on, a chill setting in.
I say a few words under my breath.
Who knows if we can handle another late frost.

EARLY EVENING, LATE OCTOBER

The backyard sycamores shed their skins like snakes,
their torsos naked in the fading light,
mirrored in the creek with the rising moon.
Woodsmoke, a tiny tornado of leaves, & tonight
the festival of souls,
the dead stepping out to stretch their legs.

Across the fence, the neighbor's Labrador wheezes,
a tumor in his throat.
He brings the ball back in his mouth
one more time, then takes a nap.
I'm putting him down,
the neighbor whispers. *Won't feel a thing.*

As the moon clears the treetops,
I picture that early evening to come when I won't feel a thing,
when I'll stroll by the creek, kick leaves, sniff smoke,
pace off this plot of earth where I was happy once,
pausing to pee
like a dog marking territory that was never his.

SECOND CHILDHOOD

Sometimes I find myself
toddling again, shaky
on my skinny little legs,
holding onto grandma's apron
to keep my balance
though she's gone forever.

Is crawling far behind?
Potty training, diapers,
someone to wash my hair
with baby shampoo, no
tears? The difference is,
this time it's me

who'll do the washing.
I'll pat my own back,
put me to bed, read me
a story. I'll sing me to sleep
& leave the night light on
for when I wake in the dark.

MUSIC

Will there be music
as we float up from our beds,
music in the air?

WHEN THIS IS ALL OVER

I'll look up at the sky
& float among the clouds,
singing out their names
like old friends I haven't seen forever.

I'll flit flower to flower,
flapping my wings so fast that no one can see them
& sticking my nose in everywhere,
sampling the nectar.

I'll lie down in a green pasture
& my arms will sprout the thorns of a thistle,
my fingers will bloom with purple petals
& you'll admire me from a safe distance.

I'll swim again in the river I was baptized in
& keep on going,
breathing through my gills & flicking my fins
as the current takes me where it will.

NOTES

The song lyrics quoted in "Homecoming" are from "I've Thought of Leaving Too" (1964) by Lee Emerson, recorded and released the same year on the album *Country Music Time* by Kitty Wells.

The song lyrics quoted in "What I'm Looking For" are from "Lush Life" (1938) by Billy Strayhorn. The recording I refer to is from the album *John Coltrane and Johnny Hartman*, recorded and released in 1963.

The mention of Oliver Lewis (1856-1924) in "Horse Capital" refers to the winning jockey in the first Kentucky Derby in 1875. Lewis, who was African-American, has a street named for him in his hometown of Lexington.

For the details of Lizzie Alcott's death in "The Bookcase," I'm indebted to Carmen Maria Machado's article "The Real Tragedy of Beth March," published in *The Paris Review* in 2019.

And a personal note: I took a long absence—almost fifteen years—from writing poetry, then found my way back to it in 2019. Since then I've been nurtured by three writing communities: Poezia, Lexington's longest-running poetry workshop; the regulars at Lexington Poetry Month; and the Blueberry Group, whose members have become some of my dearest friends: Linda Angelo, Joe Anthony, Jennifer Barricklow, Linda Bryant, Coleman Davis, Shelda Hale, Kimberly Miller, Jules Unsel, Larry Vogt and Laverne Zabielski. I love you all.

ACKNOWLEDGMENTS

My thanks to the journals and anthologies in which these poems first appeared, sometimes in different forms: *Appalachian Review*: "Back from the Funeral," "A Visitation"; *Blood Tree Literature*: "Basilisk"; *But There Was Fire in the Distance* (Lexington Poetry Month/Workhorse, 2021), ed. Pauletta Hansel: "Abecedarian for Adolescence"; *Cumberland Poetry Review*: "It," "Finishing Touches," "Dragonfly," "Afterward," "Rites of Spring"; *Literary Accents*: "Ember"; *Locks & Bones & Bells & Stamps & Maps* (Lexington Poetry Month/Workhorse, 2022), ed. Christopher McCurry: "The Napkins"; *Passager Journal*: "Wilmington"; *Pegasus*: "Jacob's Ladder," "A Sonnet, Just in Case," "Early Evening, Late October"; *Poet Lore*: "Gathering Tobacco"; *Porch Screen Review*: "What I'm Looking For"; *Reliquary*: "The Right to Remain Silent"; *Salvation South*: "Mouths to Feed"; *Something Like Sentience Scattered and Smoldering* (Lexington Poetry Month/Workhorse, 2023), eds. Arwen Careaga and Jon Thrower: "Tenancies"; *Still: The Journal*: "Mea Culpa in Lexington Cemetery"; *The Archive*: "First Light"; *The Bell*: "Last Call at Bethany Spring," "Seven Views of Owsley Fork," "When This Is All Over"; *The Lyricist*: "Tramroad"; *The North American Review*: "Smoke"; *Willawaw Journal*: "Under the Hood," "Educated Guess," "Meanwhile"; *Yearling*: "Eclipse," "Brightleaf," "Death's Door."

ABOUT THE AUTHOR

Kevin Nance is a writer, photographer and arts journalist. A North Carolinian, he was educated at Duke University and has lived for many years in Lexington, Kentucky. His poems have appeared in many literary journals including *Cumberland Poetry Review*, which awarded him the Robert Penn Warren Poetry Prize, judged by Helen Vendler, in 2003. His two collections of photographs and haiku are *Even If* (University of Kentucky Arts in HealthCare, 2020) and *Midnight* (Act of Power Press, 2022). His book of photographs, *Geneva's Garden: Four Seasons of Beauty in Lexington's Gratz Park*, was published in 2024. As an arts journalist, his work has been published in the *Washington Post*, the *Wall Street Journal*, *USA Today*, the *Chicago Tribune*, the *Chicago Sun-Times*, *Poets & Writers Magazine* and other publications. He is co-host (with Jay McCoy) of *Kentucky Writers Roundtable*, a literary interview program on RadioLex. His photography can be seen at *kevinnance.tumblr.com*.

www.ingramcontent.com/pod-product-compliance
Lightning Source LLC
Chambersburg PA
CBHW03122120626
46545CB00003B/942